The Baseball Life of
Johnny Bench

by JOHN DEVANEY

with photos

SCHOLASTIC BOOK SERVICES

NEW YORK • TORONTO • LONDON • AUCKLAND • SYDNEY • TOKYO

For the teachers and students of P.S. 3,
the second home of John and Luke.

Photo credits—United Press International—4, 33, 44, 66, 73, 79, 86, 94, 103. Wide World Photos—12, 24, 28, 51, 56.

Acknowledgements:
Most of the material in this book was obtained during interviews by me with Johnny Bench for articles in *Sport* and other magazines. I thank Johnny for his always generous help and kindness. I also owe a debt to these gentlemen who have written newspaper and magazine articles about Johnny: Earl Lawson, Bucky Pope, Bob Hertzel, Bill Libby, George Vecsey, Lou Prato, and Al Stump. — J.D.

1st printing . . . . March 1974
Printed in the U. S. A.

CONTENTS

Johnny Cool
Comes Through

JOHNNY BENCH stepped out of the dugout swinging three bats. He tossed two away and started toward home plate. A roaring as loud as the thunder of a thousand jets filled Riverfront Stadium in Cincinnati. Some 40,000 Reds fans were standing and cheering for their own Johnny Bench, begging him to hit a home run.

This was the game that would decide the 1972 National League pennant. The Reds were battling the Pittsburgh Pirates in the play-offs. Each team had won two games; the winner of this game would be the National League champions.

The Pirates led, 3-2, in the bottom of the ninth. If the Pirates could get three more outs, they would be on their way to the 1972 World Series, and Johnny Bench and the rest of the Reds could unpack their bags and stay home.

Johnny curled his long fingers around the bat. He watched Dave Giusti, the ace Pirate reliefer, warming up; he was whizzing fast balls into the catcher's mitt.

"Tough pitcher. Throws hard stuff. Can knock the bat out of your hands," Johnny said to himself.

Giusti would wing outside pitches at Johnny. As a right-handed hitter, Bench usually pulled most of his home runs over the left-field fence. But with outside fast balls, the chances were he'd slap easy grounders at the second baseman instead of home runs over the left-field fence.

"John! John!"

Johnny turned. He saw his mother standing near the screen behind home plate.

"Hit me a home run, John!" his mother seemed to be shouting. "Hit me a home run!"

Sure, but I wish it was that easy, he thought.

He turned back toward the plate. The roaring grew even louder. The fans too were clamoring for a home run. After all, he was Johnny Bench, the leading home-run hitter in the National League for two of the past three seasons.

Johnny knew how much was expected of him. Yet his gray eyes watched calmly as Giusti warmed up, and his broad face wore the far-away look of someone doing a math problem in his head.

"If I look composed," he once said, "I guess it's because I'm not naturally excitable. Some people say I don't have any nerves. Of course I do. But in an emergency I don't let my nerves take charge. One thing I will never do is panic."

Giusti finished his warm-up pitches, and Johnny stepped into the batter's box. Everyone in Riverfront Stadium was standing. The noise was deafening. Millions across the nation leaned forward to peer intently at their TV sets.

He watched the pitcher rub up the ball, and swung his bat in short arcs. Now Giusti was ready to pitch.

In zoomed a fast ball. Sure enough, it was outside. Then came a slider — again outside. The Pirates were taking no chances. They weren't going to throw an inside pitch that Johnny could jerk over the left-field wall for a game-tying home run.

The count rose to one strike and two balls.

Giusti looked down for the sign. He nodded, then went into his wind-up. He threw a palm ball that danced toward the outside edge of the plate. Johnny lashed out at the pitch. He caught the ball with the fat part of his bat.

The *crack* as he connected pierced the crowd's

Johnny Bench slugging a homer is a familiar sight around the National League as Cincinnati's ace catcher gets hold of one.

roar; the ball soared high toward the right-field wall some 375 feet from home.

Johnny raced toward first. He saw Pirate right fielder Roberto Clemente rushing toward the wall, glove outstretched. At the wall Clemente stopped and looked up. The ball was arching downward. Clemente strained toward it and then lowered his glove as the ball crashed into the right-field seats.

Home run! Home run! Home run! Reds' fans were jumping, screaming the happy words. The game was tied, 3-3. The Reds were alive. The Reds still had a chance to win the pennant.

Johnny was trotting around second base. A grin split his face. He clapped hands with the third-base coach, loped toward home, touched the plate, and trotted toward the dugout still grining. He'd slammed the biggest home run of his life!

At the dugout the Reds' players engulfed him. They hugged him, even kissed him. Johnny flopped down onto the bench, the sweat trickling down his happy face. "Let's get 'em gang," he said. "Let's win this one now...."

The Big Red Machine did just that — win this one now. Tony Perez slashed a single. George Foster ran for Perez. He dashed to second when Denis Menke lined another single into left field. Then Cesar Geronimo lofted a long fly to Clemente in right. After the catch, the speedy Foster took off from second base and slid safely into third.

Bob Moose, now pitching for the Pirates, looked down at the next hitter, Hal McRae. Moose twisted off a curve. The ball broke low into the dirt and bounded past catcher Manny Sanguillen. Foster could see the white ball hopping along the green turf — a wild pitch! He ran home. The Reds were 4-3 winners and the 1972 National League champions.

As the Reds swarmed into their carpeted clubhouse, they were screeching, laughing, slapping one another on the back. "Way to go...way to go, gang...we did it...!"

Reporters ringed Johnny, pads and pencils in hand. "I wasn't up there to hit a triple," Johnny was yelling above the pandemonium. "I wanted it to go out."

"There's our leader," second baseman Joe Morgan shouted to a reporter, pointing a thumb at Johnny. "He showed us the way. We followed him. We always follow him. That's why we call him the Little General."

"You're pretty young to be a general," a reporter said to Johnny. "How old are you — 24?"

Johnny nodded. "Yes," he said, "but I can take all the pressure they put on. A catcher has to take the pressure. That's why he has to be calm and confident, even cocky. If you're not, then you're not doing your job."

This reporter first met Johnny Bench in the visitors' clubhouse in the Astrodome in Houston. We shook hands, but as we talked about baseball, his face was somber and he showed very little friendliness.

Later though, in an interview in his high-rise apartment in Cincinnati, Johnny turned out to be very friendly. "The reason I don't smile very much," he said, "is that I chipped two front teeth when I was growing up. I thought this made me look funny. I was self-conscious about my appearance. It sort of made me reserved. My teeth are fine now. But I just got out of the habit of smiling, and I still don't smile or laugh as much as most people. There are funny things in life, and I like a good laugh as well as the next fellow. But I think I look more serious and take a more serious outlook on life than most.

"I dreaded failing," he said. "Not failing for myself, because I have confidence in what I can do. But when I was in the minor leagues and I heard people say, 'This guy is sure to be in the major leagues,' I was afraid I'd fail all those people who had said all those things about me."

Johnny had played only a few games in the minors when the great Yogi Berra — then a Met coach — saw him play. Yogi, who had once been one of baseball's best catchers, said about Johnny then, "He's only 17 but he could catch in the big leagues right now."

Late in 1967 Johnny came up from the minors to play a few games for the Reds. Managers and coaches raved about his line-drive throws to second base to cut down base stealers. Others predicted he would be one of the league's leading home-run hitters.

The following spring, the 20-year-old Johnny reported to the Reds' training camp in Tampa, Florida. One day the Reds were playing Washington. The Senators' manager was Ted Williams, the former Red Sox slugger who's now in the Hall of Fame. As Johnny tossed a ball to another Red during the pregame warm-up, he spied Williams walking toward the Senators' clubhouse. Ted Williams! As a boy Johnny had stood on dusty vacant lots, swinging at tin cans and imagining he was Ted Williams blasting another long home run. Now, he thought, here he was on the same baseball diamond with Ted Williams himself.

Johnny picked up a baseball and followed Williams into the clubhouse. The tall manager was sitting at his desk in his office, talking with a couple of newspapermen.

"Excuse me, Mr. Williams," young Johnny said, holding out the baseball. "Could I have your autograph?"

"Sure, son," Ted Williams said. He signed the ball and handed it back. "Thanks." Johnny said, flushing a little. He left the office gripping the ball.

One of the reporters turned to Williams. "How does that kid Bench look to you, Ted?"

"Was that Johnny Bench?" Williams exclaimed. "Hey, do me a favor. Go get that baseball I signed for him."

The reporter walked over to the Reds' clubhouse. "Hey, Bench," the reporter said. "Ted Williams wants that ball back."

Surprised, Johnny gave him the ball.

A few minutes later the reporter returned to the Reds' clubhouse. He was grinning. He handed the ball to Johnny, who turned it over and read the words his boyhood idol had written to him:

"To Johnny Bench — a Hall of Famer for sure. Ted Williams."

Almost certainly Johnny Lee Bench will one day enter the Hall of Fame. In 1970 he was picked as the National League's Most Valuable Player, becoming, at 22, the youngest player ever to win the award. By age 24, Johnny had won the MVP award twice, after being picked as the league's Most Valuable Player again in 1972.

Only five other big leaguers have won the MVP award twice — at any age. Three of those — Carl Hubbell, Stan Musial, and Roy Campanella — are enshrined in the Hall of Fame. The two others — Ernie Banks and Willie Mays — are sure to join them one day in the Hall.

Only Stan Musial and Roy Campanella have won the National League's MVP award three times. And, as Johnny can look forward to at least 10 more years in the big leagues, he will also have the opportunity to win the award three times, or even four, or more.

But the road to the Hall of Fame is not without its pitfalls. In 1971 Johnny hit only .238, and

Cincinnati fans booed him lustily. Some called him a flash-in-the-pan. "He was good for a couple of years," the fans said, "but now the pitchers have him figured out."

Johnny tried to shrug off the booing. But he was hurt. "I guess," he said a year later, "if you could look into my mind, you would find the scars from last year still there someplace."

The joy and glory of being a big-league catcher, however, more than made up for the hurt. Johnny had yearned to be a big-league catcher from way back, from the days when he sat in a second-grade class in Binger, Oklahoma.

"I dreamed of being Mickey Mantle because he was from Oklahoma," Johnny once said. "I dreamed of being Ted Williams. I dreamed of being this guy or that guy. I dreamed of breaking big-league records. I grew up on dreams."

They Laughed at Johnny

THE YELLOW BUS chugged up the hill, carrying the Binger High School baseball team home from a game. Inside the bus the 10 Binger players were talking. They had just beaten the Riverside Indian School.

Binger won most of its games. It had the best high school pitcher in those parts — a chesty boy named Johnny Lee Bench. In two years, Johnny had lost only one game. And he could hit. He was the best hitter on the team, batting around .600.

At the moment he was sitting in the middle of the bus next to his pal, Davey Gunther. Suddenly he felt the bus tilt on the peak of the hill and start plunging downhill. The bus was picking up speed — too much speed.

In batting cage before a game, Bench displays his great power of concentration: eye on ball and following through.

Someone yelled. Someone else screamed.

The driver, coach Lloyd Dinse, jammed hard on the brake pedal, but the bus didn't slow down. The brakes had failed!

As Johnny saw the roadside shooting by, he remembered what his father had told him to do in an emergency:

Hit the deck!

So Johnny grabbed Davey Gunther and they hit the deck, dropping to the floor of the bus. Johnny flopped over Davey, protecting him.

He heard the other boys screaming. The bus sped down the hill toward an intersection. Beyond the intersection yawned a deep ravine.

Coach Dinse tugged at the wheel. The bus

tilted sharply on its side wheels. It toppled, tumbling down the side of the steep hill. Metal screeched against rock, glass shattered, tires burst.

Inside the bus the boys were thrown from their seats in wild confusion. Legs and arms stabbed through glass windows. Screams mingled with the sound of twisting metal. Johnny's head struck something. For a moment he was unconscious.

He woke to see his feet sticking through the side of a shattered window. The bus had rolled upright at the bottom of the hill and steam, hissing from the broken radiator, mixed with the choking dust. Boys cried in pain, gripping their broken arms and legs. The bodies of two boys were twisted awkwardly amid the wrecked seats. They were dead.

Johnny got up slowly, still slightly dazed, and stared in horror. Then he checked himself. He had only a small cut on his elbow. Blood trickled from a few slashes in Davey's arms. At least he'd saved his seatmate and himself from bad injury.

In an emergency Johnny had thought fast. He hadn't panicked — and nothing ever would make him panic after this. He had done what his father had taught him to do — hit the deck.

Johnny had been doing what his father, Ted,

had taught him to do ever since he could remember. Johnny was born on December 7, 1947, in Oklahoma City. His mother and father are of mixed Dutch, English, Irish, and Indian ancestry. Johnny's great-grandmother had been a Choctaw Indian. That makes Johnny one eighth Indian. He is quietly proud of his Indian heritage. "In a way," his father told Johnny, "Indians are the only real Americans."

Johnny's dad had been a catcher for a semiprofessional team. He was paid only two or three dollars a game. Ted Bench drove a truck during the day and played the game he loved at night and on weekends until in one game he injured a hand and had to give up baseball.

Down the drain went his hopes of being a bigleague catcher. He decided he would try to make his sons what he could not be: a big-league catcher.

Ted had three sons and a daughter, Marilyn, who was the youngest of the family. The oldest was Ted. Then came Bill. Johnny was the youngest boy. When the boys were tots, their father bought gloves, bats, and balls for them. In the evenings he pitched batting practice to the older boys and played catch with young Johnny.

When Johnny was four, his father moved the family to Binger, a small town of about 600 people. Binger, nestled among rolling hills a few miles south of Oklahoma City, was eight blocks long and eight blocks wide, and ringed about by farms.

The Bench family lived in a stucco house in Binger Center. Little Johnny and his pals played in a nearby dusty lot. His father glowed when he saw how Johnny swung at the battered baseballs. It was plain to see that the boy loved to play ball. His older sons had never showed the passion for the game that Johnny did.

At night Mr. Bench would talk to Johnny about the great catchers: Bill Dickey, Mickey Cochrane, Yogi Berra. He showed his son how to crouch behind hitters, how to catch low pitches, how to straighten and throw out runners. Johnny's eyes gleamed as he listened. Maybe some day he could catch like Bill Dickey.

When Johnny was in the second grade, his teacher asked each of her students to stand up and say what he or she hoped to be.

"A rancher," said one boy.

"A policeman," said another.

Johnny stood up. In his solemn way he announced, "I want to be a big-league catcher."

The class laughed as Johnny sat down, but he meant what he'd said. Some day, when he repeated it, they would not laugh.

Already, Johnny could hit a ball harder and throw it farther than any of his friends. One reason was that his friends went off to swim, bicycle, or just fool around, while Johnny stayed on the dusty lot, under a broiling sun, and worked to make himself a better ballplayer. He made up games he could play by himself.

Johnny would pick up a tennis ball and throw it at the propane-gas tank in the back of his house. The ball would strike the side of the tank and carom off. He would dash to his left and scoop up the bouncing ball. He imagined himself throwing to first. The batter was out!

This was one of his favorite games. Later he described how he played it:

"First, I'd pretend I was the batter. Usually I imagined I was Mickey Mantle. He was a star for the Yankees then and, like me, he was from Oklahoma. I'd throw the tennis ball at the tank. Then I'd be the fielder, trying to catch the ball before it got by a certain point. If I caught it, the batter was out. If I didn't catch it, the ball was a single, double, triple, or home run, depending on how far the ball went...."

For instance, Johnny would imagine it was the last of the ninth, with the Yankees tied, 3-3, with the Red Sox. "Mickey's up," Johnny would say. Then he'd throw the tennis ball at the gas tank, aiming the ball so that it caromed off the tank at a crazy angle. Johnny would chase after the bounding ball. If he couldn't snare it, if it bounced four, five, six times, it was a home run for Mickey Mantle, and the Yankees had won the game.

Johnny would smile to himself, picking up the tennis ball. He'd thrown that ball so there had been no way he could have fielded it.

When Johnny and his friends couldn't find enough boys for a game of nine-man baseball, they made up the game of Tin Can. They sawed an old baseball bat down the middle to form one flat side. Then they punched holes in a small milk can. The can was their ball. If the boy whacked the can a certain distance, he had hit a single. If he clipped it farther, it was a double, triple, or home run.

Years later Johnny was telling a friend about those games of Tin Can. "After you hit that can 20 or 30 times with the flat bat, the can would be battered to the size of a half dollar. And with those holes in it, the can would break and dip like a curve ball. It was real tough to hit. Swinging at those swerving cans taught me how to hit the curve and slider."

Ted Bench watched his son Johnny pitch, catch, play infield and outfield. But what he wanted was to have Johnny concentrate on catching.

"There's always a shortage of good catchers in the big leagues," he told Johnny. "That's because it takes a lot more ability to be a good catcher."

This former semipro catcher gave his youngest son a score of tips on catching. "It's a long throw from home plate to second base to catch a runner stealing," he told Johnny. "It's 127 feet or so. But you should practice throwing the ball 250 feet. Then when you have to throw 127 feet in a game, it won't seem so far."

He taught Johnny to aim at targets when he threw the ball 250 feet, and to focus on a glove or the knee of the boy to whom he was throwing. He showed the boy how to grip the ball across the seams to add velocity to his throws.

Ted Bench knew that practice wasn't enough to make his son a big-league catcher. Johnny would have to play in real games. Binger was too small a town to field a Little League team. Johnny's father dipped into his thin savings and bought equipment for nine players. He scheduled games with teams in nearby towns. He piled his Binger Bobcats on the back of his truck and drove them to the games.

Nine-year-old Johnny pitched, caught, and played third base, first, and the outfield. "But everyone knows," he once said, "that I am going to be a catcher."

He won most of the games he pitched, zipping fast balls by the hitters. And he was the team's clean-up hitter, slamming at least one home run in almost every game played.

When Johnny was 10, he pitched and caught for the nearby Fort Cobb Little League team. His father drove him to the games. In two years he pitched more than a dozen no-hitters.

"You could be a good pitcher if you wanted to," his father told Johnny one day.

"Maybe," Johnny said, "but a pitcher gets to play only every four days. I want to play every day. I want to catch."

Johnny was knocking off one or two home runs a game. "He's so small," people said. "How does he hit all those homers?"

Johnny was about average size for his age. He was five-foot-two and weighed about 100 pounds. "But he's as strong as this," his father would say, holding a steel bar. Besides, Johnny had enormous hands. His friends, in fact, nick-named him Hands.

But Johnny kept wishing he were taller and heavier. And when he was in the ninth grade, that wish came true. He shot up eight inches, to five-foot-10, and made the high school baseball and basketball teams. On a basketball court Johnny could leap high enough to stuff the ball through the hoop. In one season he averaged 24 points and 17 rebounds a game. The Binger basketball team went to the state finals each year, but there they lost to taller teams.

"I love basketball," Johnny told a friend one

day. "But I never forget what I have set my mind on — to be a big-league catcher."

As a pitcher for Binger High, Johnny won more than 30 games, and lost only two. Those two games were lost when his teammates booted balls, allowing unearned runs to score. At bat Johnny hit .675. In one game he cracked four home runs.

In the classroom Johnny got A's and B's. Yet he never had to study hard. His mind soaked up facts quickly. He used that mind to learn the trade of catching. He watched big-league catchers being interviewed on TV, and copied their tips on catching in a notebook. Each night he studied those notes and soon had them memorized.

Life wasn't all sports for Johnny. When he was 12, he worked in the cotton fields during school vacations. From dawn to dusk he picked cotton, crawling on his knees in 110-degree heat.

"You could get a drink of water only at the end of each row, which was about a quarter-mile long," he once recalled. "And the water wasn't cold.

"You'd pull a sack behind you and dump it off at the end of the row when it was full. I could pull two, three, four hundred pounds a day. They paid only two cents a pound, but if I could get 400 pounds, that was eight dollars. It was enough to buy my own levis and shirts and things like that. But it was hot, sweaty, dirty work."

After work or play, though, there was the good Oklahoma rural life. "I can remember Dad coming home with a watermelon for all of us to dig into. I can remember Mom making ice cream out back. I can remember running through warm, open fields on summer evenings. I can remember sliding down snowy slopes...."

But that life was coming to an end. Big-league scouts were streaming into Binger to talk to Johnny. They watched him throw and hit, and wrote reports to their teams raving about Johnny Bench. They talked to him about signing a contract to play in the minor leagues. But first he had to be graduated from high school. He was the class valedictorian and gave the farewell address at the graduation ceremonies.

A few weeks before graduation a teacher again asked some of the 22 boys and girls in Johnny's class what they planned to be.

"A nurse," said a girl.

"A truck driver," said a boy.

"A big-league catcher," said Johnny Bench. That time, no one laughed.

"I Was Scared..."

"ARE YOU PITCHING today, John?"

"Yes," Johnny Bench said. He was talking to a scout from the St. Louis Cardinals a few minutes before a high school game.

It was in the spring of 1965, just a few weeks before graduation, after which any big-league team could draft Johnny to play for them.

"Well, even if you are pitching," the scout said, "I'd like to see you throw from home plate to second base."

"Sure," Johnny said. Before the game started, he put on catching gear, crouched behind the plate, took a throw from a pitcher, and whipped the ball to the second baseman. Then he took off the gear and went to the mound. He pitched a three-hitter to win the game, 3-0, driving in two of the runs with two home runs.

The Cardinals' scout was talking to a Reds' scout after the game. "He has a great arm," said the Reds' scout. "He could be a pitcher or a catcher. And he can hit home runs."

"Oh, he can hit," the Cardinals' scout answered. "Johnny says his father taught him to catch, but hitting came natural to him. But can he hit real good pitching? Playing in a small town like Binger, he hasn't seen a lot of strong pitching."

In big-league offices across the country, club officials were studying the scouting reports on Bench and hundreds of other high school and college players. In a few days the club officials would gather in New York to pick the best of these players for their teams. The lower-standing teams would go first. Each club would pick one player. Then there would be a second round with each club again picking one player. There would be many more rounds until all the young players had been chosen. A player could sign only with a team that had picked or "drafted" him.

As with all the other club officials, a Reds' official went through a process of elimination before the first round. He liked Johnny Bench's

Johnny welcomes mother, father, and sister, Marilyn, as they come to New York to watch him make a special TV program.

record. But he also liked the record of Bernie Carbo, a 17-year-old third baseman from Garden City, Michigan. He finally decided: "We'll pick Carbo on the first round. He's hit against better pitching than Bench."

Then the actual picking began. On the first round the clubs picked people like Bernie Carbo, outfielder Rick Monday, pitcher Joe Coleman, infielder Alex Barrett, outfielder Billy Conigliaro. Some of them would become famous; others would never make it to the big leagues.

Not one of the 20 major-league clubs had picked Johnny Bench in the first round.

The second round began. The A's, Senators,

Mets, Astros, Braves, Red Sox, Cubs, Indians, Dodgers, Twins, Pirates, Angels, Tigers, Giants, and Orioles all skipped Johnny. Only one of the players they chose, pitcher Allan Foster, ever made it to the big leagues. Yet any one of those 15 teams could have picked a winner, Johnny Bench. Johnny was finally chosen by the 16th team — the Cincinnati Reds.

A few days later he signed with the Reds for $10,000. Rick Monday and other players picked in the first round had signed for as much as $100,000. "I'm happy to get $10,000," Johnny told friends. "It's more money, by far, than we have ever had in the bank before."

Johnny was told to report to the Reds' Class A minor-league team in Tampa, Florida. So one evening in late June of 1965 he drove with his family to the airport in Oklahoma City. He walked up a ramp to a plane, waved good-bye to his parents and brothers and sister, and a few minutes later he was on his way.

At about 8:00 P.M., Johnny looked down and saw the twinkling lights of Tampa. Off to his left the lights blazed on Al Lopez Field, where the Tampa Tarpons were playing that night.

Johnny had been told to go directly to the ball park. There he was handed a uniform and told to put it on quickly. Johnny dressed, picked up his mitt and walked from the clubhouse to the dugout. The Tarpon manager shook his hand. "We're short of catchers," he told him. "Go out there and catch the last of the ninth."

Johnny had wanted action, but he hadn't expected to walk off the plane into a game. It was a frightened 17-year-old who trotted out to the plate, slipped on a mask, and crouched to give signals to a grown man, an experienced player. But Johnny hid his fright and got through the inning. Afterward, he went with the team to a hotel in Tampa, unpacked, and fell asleep. In one night he had traveled a thousand miles from his country home to a big city, and played in a minor league game. It was overwhelming.

The next morning when he awoke, he looked out the window and thought: I'm only 17. What am I doing here, trying to play pro ball? "I was scared," he said years later.

In the clubhouse the next night, Johnny heard the older players laughing at him. He talked like a country boy. He acted like a country boy. And when he tried to get friendly, he stammered and said stupid things. Then he blushed, his ears tingling, and the other players laughed.

Some of the older players who were making fun of him were really jealous. They had heard about his $10,000 bonus. "Hey, country boy," they shouted at Johnny in the clubhouse. "Where do you keep your money — in your socks?"

Johnny wanted to slink off by himself. But he was the team's number-one catcher. Each game he had to step out in front of the plate, fist clenched, and encourage his pitchers. He had to be the leader. But the older men sneered at a mere kid trying to act the leader. Johnny began to dread going to the park.

One night Johnny decided to phone his parents in Binger. He didn't mention his feelings, but they were in his voice when he told his father he was hitting around .250 and playing every day.

"Good," his father said, "keep up the good work." After hanging up, though, Ted Bench told his wife that Johnny had sounded homesick. At three o'clock the next morning the Benches started on the thousand-mile drive to Tampa. Johnny's face brightened when he saw them. When they left, a few days later, he had come to realize what he had to do.

"I realized this was a man's job," he said later. "It was no place for a boy. I was in a man's position, drawing a man's salary. A good salary. There was no reason why I shouldn't do my job....I had to go from being a boy to being a man overnight."

That year Johnny hit .248 and stroked two home runs. But statistics did not tell the full story.

"He's smart, strong, and a winning-type ball-

In hospital for surgery to remove a spot on his lung, Johnny turns things around to take pulse of the nurse, Paula Riemar.

player," one Reds' scout told club officials in Cincinnati. "And what an arm!"

In 1966 Bench was jumped to the Peninsula team in the Carolina League. He smacked 22 home runs. In one game, in a single inning, he threw out three base stealers. Rex Bowen, a Pirate scout, said of him: "He's the best right-handed hitter I've seen break into baseball since Joe DiMaggio. He's only 18 and he could catch right now in the big leagues."

The Reds promoted him at midseason to Buffalo — their top minor-league team. Then in the first inning of his first game at Buffalo, a foul tip broke his right thumb.

A dejected Johnny flew home to Binger, finished for the season. Some friends from Binger were playing a tournament in Wichita, Kansas. Johnny drove to Wichita to watch them play.

Returning, Johnny was cruising down a wide highway. Suddenly he saw another car weaving toward him. Headlights flashed in his eyes.

The car was in the wrong lane.

The driver was drunk, and Johnny swerved — too late. The other car rammed into the side of his car with a shattering roar. Broken glass ripped open Johnny's head — and his left arm. The blood gushed from his arm as he fought the car to a screeching stop.

He slumped over the wheel. Then a voice was saying, "Easy, let me help you...."

A doctor had been driving behind Johnny; now he was trying to staunch the flow of blood. "Get him to a hospital right away," the doctor told a policeman, who arrived minutes later.

A siren wailed from afar. An ambulance slammed to a stop. Attendants gently lifted Johnny into the ambulance, and it roared away, tires squealing.

Inside the ambulance Johnny stared at the roof. His head and arm ached. He looked down at his blood-splotched arm. Would he end up as a cripple, he wondered. Would he ever play baseball again?

The Holler Guy

"YOU'RE NEVER GOING to make it to the big leagues that way, son," the Buffalo coach said, shaking his head.

Johnny, crouching behind the plate, glanced at the coach. "You mean because I'm catching one-handed?"

"That's right."

"It's the safe way to catch," Johnny said. He had come to the Buffalo team's training camp in Florida in the spring of 1967, after recovering from the auto accident. Doctors had sewed some 20 stitches in his head and arm, but he wasn't crippled, as he had feared. "I'm lucky to be alive," he told people, thinking about the over-turned bus and then the auto collision.

Over the winter Johnny had thought a lot about how injuries to a catcher's bare hand could end his career. That had happened to his father.

That won't happen to me, Johnny decided.

He decided to learn to catch the ball one-handed with his mitt. He'd keep his bare hand behind his back, or at his side, protecting the hand from foul tips.

Johnny bought a new, lighter catcher's mitt. With his big hand he could squeeze the mitt and catch a ball.

"Oh, you can catch the ball all right in the mitt," the Buffalo coach was telling Johnny. "But suppose a runner is breaking for second, trying to steal? By the time you get the ball out of the glove and get re/dy to throw, he'll be at second base."

"Randy Hundley of the Cubs catches one-handed," replied Johnny.

"He's the only one in the big leagues who does. The Giants owned him. They traded him to the Cubs. They didn't think he could make it in the big leagues catching one-handed. And I don't think he will either."

Johnny went on practicing his one-handed catching. For hours, over and over again, he whipped the ball out of the mitt and cocked to throw. Early in the season he said: "By now I don't even think about it. No matter how the ball comes into the glove, I've got it across the seams by the time I've pulled it out of the mitt and I'm ready to throw. One-handed catching looks flashy, but actually I find it more efficient."

Speedy baserunners were taking off, trying to steal second against the 19-year-old Buffalo catcher. Most good baserunners will steal second base seven out of every 10 tries. Against Johnny the runners were successful fewer than five out of every 10 tries.

"I can throw out any base stealer alive," Johnny told a reporter.

The word spread around the league: Johnny Bench is the boastful, show-off kind.

"I know you're supposed to act humble when you're being complimented," Johnny told friends. "But I don't believe in that. I know what I can do. If you're not cocky as a catcher, you're not doing your job."

Bench had changed after two years of rattling around in minor-league buses. He had lived in run-down hotels and rooming houses. He knew what it was like to be alone in strange towns. He had taken on a man's job. And now he was a man.

In the clubhouse he didn't say much. His big face was usually solemn, his gray eyes unblinking, taking in everything that was happening around him.

But on the field Johnny was a holler guy. "Shake it up, this is no Sunday picnic," he shouted at his infielders. "Bend your back and throw your hard stuff," he snapped at his pitchers when they tried to take it easy. "Come on,

One month after lung surgery, Bench is on way to recovery, as
he drives off tee in annual golf classic sponsored by airline.

we can win this one," he yelled in the dugout, clapping his hands, when Buffalo came to bat in the late innings.

Early in the season Johnny wasn't slamming too many hits. But he kept on throwing out base stealers. "You don't let your hitting problems hurt your fielding," he told the other players. And he went on being the holler guy, exhorting the other players to get hits even when he himself wasn't getting hits.

By June of the 1967 season, however, Johnny had adjusted his swing to meet the fast balls of International League pitchers. He began to bang long home runs. In two months he had rapped 17 homers.

His parents drove from Binger to Buffalo to see him play. Katie and Ted Bench were sitting in the stands when they heard the announcer's voice over the public-address system:

"Now batting fourth for Buffalo...." Johnny stepped in. A high fast ball arrowed toward him. He swung. The crowd roared. Mr. and Mrs. Bench stood up, watching the ball streak toward the left-field fence.

Home run! It was the first home run they had seen Johnny hit as a professional. Later someone gave the ball to Johnny and he gave it to his parents. "That home run was one of the biggest thrills Johnny has ever given his mother and me," Johnny's father said years later.

During that 1967 International League season, Bench had hit 23 home runs, with a batting average of .259. He led the league's catchers in throwing out base stealers. *The Sporting News* named him "Minor League Player of the Year."

That year, 1967, the Cincinnati Reds were battling to finish fourth in the National League. They called on Bench to help in the closing month of the season. Johnny flew from Buffalo to Cincinnati. He felt nervous as he walked into his first big-league clubhouse. He was only 19 years old and here he stood among players like Pete Rose and catcher Johnny Edwards, players he had watched on television.

Then he saw Dave Bristol, the Reds' manager. Bristol had coached him in the minor leagues. Bristol walked over to Johnny. He shook hands. And then he said, "You're my number-one catcher."

Johnny stared. He couldn't believe it. He walked over to a stall and began to take off his shirt, his fingers numbed by shock. Johnny Edwards and the other catcher, Don Pavletich, were glaring at him. This rookie from the minor leagues had walked in and — just like that — had taken away the job from two veterans.

Johnny was cocky. But this was too much even for him. He was only two years out of high school, he reminded himself. He'd always thought he would make it to the big leagues.

"But I never thought it would happen this fast," he said to himself.

He looked around. He hoped someone would come over and say hello. He was too scared to speak first to anyone.

He thought about what he had done so far in baseball. People had raved about him. But, heck, he'd never hit for a high average. He made a lot of errors. He wasn't as slick a receiver as he would like to be. He was still mastering the trick of being a one-handed catcher. He had to learn to relax at the plate. He had to swing the bat with more confidence....

Panic rose in Johnny's chest. *He was the number-one catcher for a big-league team...he, Johnny Bench, who had been catching for Binger High on an Oklahoma sandlot only two years ago....It was scary....*

Johnny pushed down the fear. He knew that a lot of the players thought he was a brash rookie, too big for his britches. But he had a job to do and he was going to go out there and do it.

In the game that day he surprised the Red infielders with the power of his throws. "You see the ball coming so low," said shortstop Woody Woodward after the game, "and you are sure you are going to have to one-hop it. But it keeps right on coming, never more than two feet off the ground, and it explodes on you."

"It's a heavy ball he throws," said second

baseman Tommy Helms. "It stings you."

The other Red catchers were not impressed. They huddled together in a corner of the clubhouse. Johnny saw them talking among themselves. He knew what they were talking about: him. "The kid's hitting about .150," one of the catchers was saying to another. "He has trouble stopping low pitches. How can the skipper keep him in the lineup every day?"

"Beats me."

Cincinnati newspaperman Earl Lawson saw the catchers muttering. Lawson smelled trouble. Other Reds' players were siding with the catchers against Johnny and Manager Bristol, dividing the team.

"Dave Bristol thinks this kid can be a great catcher and hitter for the Reds," Lawson told Pete Rose, the unofficial leader of the Reds. "But he won't help this team if he's snubbed. No one can play at their best if he's lonely and thinks nobody likes him."

Rose promised he would try to befriend Johnny.

But he didn't get the chance — not that season. Two days before the end of the season Johnny was eyeing a runner taking a long lead off first base. So far Johnny had picked off several big-league runners. He called for a pitchout.

The pitch whistled in, wide of the plate.

Johnny reached for the pitch with his mitt, his bare hand coming up to pluck the ball out of the mitt. The batter swung at the pitch and ticked it. The ball glanced off Johnny's bare hand, splitting open the thumb. Bent in pain, Johnny had to leave the game.

"I tried to reach for the ball too fast," Johnny said in the clubhouse. "I won't do that again."

"Nothing serious," a doctor told Johnny. "You'll be fine next season. Go home and rest the hand."

Johnny went home to Binger. He had helped in a small way to lift the Reds into a fourth-place finish. He had hit only .163 and popped only one home run in that month of big-league catching. He told himself he would hit for a higher average with more experience. "Every league I've been in," he told his father, "I've started slow as a hitter. I've been moved up so fast I had to get used to the pitching...."

But to himself, Johnny wondered: How could he be confident when he saw the Reds' catchers whispering about every pitch he called? How could he make friends with the Reds' players?

A Banner over Binger

"HEY, CORKHEAD!"

Johnny turned to see who had called him Corkhead. He was sitting in the Reds' clubhouse in Tampa on a warm spring day in 1968. The other players were dressing.

He saw Pete Rose grinning at him. "Hey, Corkhead," Pete said again. "That's what I'm going to call you, Bench. Corkhead. You got a head so big it looks like it popped out of a bottle."

Some of the Reds laughed. Johnny flushed, not too pleased about being called Corkhead. But Pete Rose was the leader of this team. If Pete Rose gave you a nickname, that meant he liked you. And if Pete liked you, some other players would like you too. The Reds followed their leader.

But Johnny knew he would have to prove himself on the field before the Reds would respect him as their number-one catcher. "Respect comes in a gradual way," a coach told Johnny one day. "You tell a pitcher to throw a fast ball and he strikes out a hitter, and that pitcher says to himself, 'Hey, that catcher knows something.' Or you move a third baseman a few feet and he makes a great play and he says to himself, 'Hey, that catcher is good.' It takes time."

Early in the 1968 season the Reds were playing the Dodgers. In the Dodger half of the sixth, Ron Fairly led off with a slashing double down the right-field line. The next batter was Tom Haller.

Crouched behind the plate, Johnny figured that Haller would try to bunt to move Fairly to third base.

Johnny signaled for a pitch wide of the plate — a pitch Haller couldn't bunt.

In came the pitch. Haller flicked his bat at the pitch and missed. Johnny grabbed the ball and snapped a line-drive throw to second base. Fairly had started toward third base. Seeing Haller miss the bunt, he tried to scramble back to second. But the ball was waiting for him. One out.

Haller walked. Red pitcher Teddy Davidson threw a wild pitch that ricocheted around the gate behind home plate. Haller sped around second base and galloped toward third.

Johnny picked up the ball at the gate. He whirled. On one knee he threw to third — a beeline throw that arrived a second before Haller. The third baseman slapped the ball on the sliding Haller.

Two out — and both outs were Johnny's work.

On the next pitch the batter bunted the ball along the first-base line. Johnny ran up the line. He scooped up the ball and lined it past the runner's ear. The ball smacked into the first baseman's mitt. *Three out.*

Johnny ran toward the dugout. "You got all three outs," one Red player said to Johnny. "Nice going."

Johnny grinned and said thanks.

The Red players were beginning to accept him. They were beginning to think, "Hey, that catcher is good, that catcher knows something."

In another game, veteran Jim Maloney was pitching for the Reds. Big Jim had hurled a no-hitter in the big leagues when Johnny was in high school. Big Jim decided he wasn't taking any orders from this kid catcher. Big Jim was calling his own game.

The count went to one ball and two strikes on

a hitter. Big Jim decided he would throw a curve.

He looked down and saw Johnny signal for a fast ball.

Big Jim shook his head. He wanted to throw the curve. Again Bench signaled for the fast ball. Face red with anger, Big Jim nodded. He wound up and threw the fast ball. It sailed by the hitter for a called third strike.

Big Jim stomped to the dugout. He threw down his glove on the bench and spun to face Johnny. "You got away with it — this time," he growled. "Don't try it again!"

Johnny spoke calmly, pleasantly. "The guy froze up," he said. "He was so surprised to see the fast ball he didn't even move his bat on that third strike."

"Yeah, I noticed," Big Jim said grudgingly. He too began to think: Maybe this kid knows something.

Other Red pitchers seemed amazed when they talked about Johnny. "He knows all the hitters already," relief pitcher Clay Carroll was saying one day in the clubhouse. "He's smart. He observes. I tell him, 'You just give me the signs and I'll throw what you ask me to throw.' I know he'll mix up the pitches real well."

One day Johnny signaled second baseman Tommy Helms to move a few feet to his right.

The next batter hit a line drive right at Tommy. Some of the players began calling Bench the Little General. "That's what he is back there when he moves us around — the Little General," first baseman Lee May said, laughing.

Opposing managers were not laughing. They were talking about Johnny with awe in their voices. Said the veteran Dodger manager Walter Alston: "Bench is the best young catcher I've seen come into the league."

In a Red-Cub game early in the season, the Cubs' Lou Johnson stood on second with two out. The next hitter, Don Kissinger, lashed a line drive into right field.

Pete Rose ran in to scoop up the ball. He saw Johnson whirling for home. He threw the ball on one hop toward home plate.

Johnny saw the play was going to be close. He lunged for the ball with his mitt hand, grabbed the ball, spun, and tagged out the sliding Johnson.

"What a tag!" Cub manager Leo Durocher growled later to reporters. "I never saw anything like that play. That Bench handled that big catcher's mitt like it was a handkerchief. You'd expect to see a tag like that made by a shortstop or a second baseman — a one-handed tag. He has the biggest hands I've ever seen on a man six feet tall. And he moves like a cat."

In a special "world series" of all-around competition for pro athletes, Bench tries tennis, loses to hockey ace Rod Gilbert.

44

"Best arm I ever saw hung on a catcher," said former Dodger shortstop Pee Wee Reese, who had caught the throws of Hall-of-Famer Roy Campanella.

"Every player has a weakness," San Diego manager Preston Gomez told a friend. "But I look and can't find one in Bench."

By now nearly all the Red players were friendly toward Johnny. They knew that his kind of throwing and catching would help them win the pennant.

But the Red catchers were still muttering about Johnny. "Look what he's hitting — only .200 or so," they told the other Red players. "A catcher's got to be a good hitter."

Manager Dave Bristol said he wasn't concerned about Johnny's weak hitting.

"This is his history. He always starts slowly," Dave said. "We may have rushed him up the ladder from the minors too fast. He has to make adjustments. But he will. He always comes on fast late in the season."

Johnny failed to get a hit in 12 consecutive times at bat. He came up to hit against the Giants in a game in May. The score was tied in the 11th inning. The bases were loaded. Johnny slapped a single through the middle to win the game.

Johnny thought he would start stroking more hits. Instead he was blanked again for 12 consecutive at-bats. The Reds were battling the Dodgers in a deadlocked extra-inning game when Johnny came to bat in the 16th inning.

He figured the Dodger pitcher would try to snake a curve ball by him. As a rookie Johnny saw a lot of puzzling curve balls. This time Johnny timed the break of the pitch, hitting it solidly. The ball caromed off the left-field fence. Bench slid into second base with the double that beat the Dodgers.

He drove home 21 runs during May. By mid-season his average hovered above .250. He finished second in the voting for the All-Star team behind the Cubs' Randy Hundley. Johnny played only a few innings in the All-Star game. But he wasn't disappointed. He was happy and proud to be there.

Only a few years earlier he had been imagining he was Mickey Mantle. Now here he was standing behind a batting cage watching Mickey Mantle hit. He sat in the same dugout with Hank Aaron and Roberto Clemente and Willie Mays. It was his favorite dream come true.

By August Johnny's average had soared to .283. He had been hitting seventh in the batting order. Bristol raised him to fifth.

"I'd like to have a shot at hitting fourth," Johnny told one of the coaches. "I could drive in more runs."

"I admire your nerve," the coach replied.

"But Bristol may think you're rushing things. I'll ask him."

Bristol nodded when the coach told him what Johnny had said. "I'll think about it," he said.

In the next three days Johnny slammed six hits, including his 14th home run. "You're hitting fourth," Bristol told him.

As the team's clean-up hitter, Johnny helped the Reds to finish in fourth place. He ended the season with a .275 average, 15 homers, and 82 runs-batted-in. Batting fourth had helped him, Johnny said. "The more pressure I have on me down the stretch," he said, "the better."

Johnny Bench had caught in 154 of the Reds' 162 games, a record number of games for a rookie catcher. "Most rookie catchers have to sit on the bench and study the hitters," a Red coach explained. "Johnny went out and learned on the job."

He led the league's catchers in put-outs. "That's because he made so many tag plays at home," the coach said. And Johnny led the league's catchers in assists. "He got an assist for every base stealer he cut down," said the coach, "and there's no one better in this league in cutting down base stealers."

There was talk that Johnny might win the league's Rookie of the Year award. No catcher had ever won the award because rookie catchers play so little.

Johnny grinned when he heard the talk. "I've checked over the past winners," he said. "No catcher has ever won it."

But a few weeks later he was sitting with his father and mother in their stucco house in Binger when the phone rang. Johnny picked up the receiver. The caller told him the news: Johnny Bench had become the first catcher in big-league history to win the Rookie of the Year award.

Johnny's pals in Binger strung up a banner. It read:

BINGER—HOME OF JOHNNY BENCH
ROOKIE OF THE YEAR

Johnny's Mother Has a Dream

"YOU HAD a great year as a rookie, John," the reporter said. He and Johnny were talking in the Reds' dugout in Tampa during spring training in 1969. "A lot of players have terrible second years. You know, they call it the sophomore jinx. Are you worried about the sophomore jinx?"

Johnny Bench studied the board flooring of the dugout. "The first year is a tough test," he said. "But the second year is a tougher test. That's when everyone is looking at you. A lot of players never repeat a good first year. The great players get better. I figure the second year is when I should show how good I really can be."

He smiled at the reporter. "I guess that

sounds conceited. I don't think I'm conceited. I just know what I can do. If I feel I can do something, I'm not afraid to say it. That's my way. It doesn't hurt anyone, except maybe myself. It puts pressure on me. But the pressure helps me. It challenges me. It gives me a goal to go for."

"Walter Alston says you'll be the All-Star catcher for the next 10 years," said the reporter.

"It's always nice to hear that kind of talk. A lot of nice things have been written about me, but I'm not going to sit back and gloat. Those clippings can't go up and hit for you."

Johnny's face was somber now. "I hope people will be saying nice things about me 10 years from now. That's when it will count."

Johnny excused himself and went out to warm up. The reporter saw Red trainer Bill Cooper sitting on the bench and went over to talk to him about Johnny.

"You don't see many guys in baseball with a build like his," Cooper said. (Johnny now measured six-foot-one and weighed 210 pounds.) "Pro football gets those types. I would say that Johnny could pin almost any guy on this team in arm wrestling."

Out on the field Johnny was joking with several teammates. One challenged him to try to hold six baseballs in his hand at one time. Johnny carefully placed the six baseballs in his

A crack photographer, Johnny often takes his camera on out-of-town trips to get pictures of opposing stars before game.

pawlike right hand. "Wow," said a player. "Never thought I'd see that done."

The disgruntled Red catchers had been traded. The Reds' number-two catcher was now Pat Corrales, who was proud to be the back-up man to Johnny. "He's the best in the business," Corrales said. With his home runs and his catching, Johnny was joining Pete Rose as the team leader.

In the game that afternoon with Houston, Gary Nolan was hurling for the Reds. In the bottom of the sixth, with the score 0-0, Nolan walked Houston's lead-off man Curt Blefary. Johnny called time and walked out to talk to Nolan.

"You're working too fast," he said to the sweating pitcher. "Instead of striding toward me, you're toppling off to the side. Get back to staying on top with your arm as you follow through."

Nolan wiped his forehead on his sleeve. He grinned weakly. "Whatever you say, General."

On the next pitch Nolan strode forward. He threw a buzzing fast ball. The batter rapped it to the shortstop, who started a successful double-play.

The Reds won the game, 4-1. In the clubhouse the players clustered around Nolan, congratulating him. Nolan smiled, thanked them, then wended his way through the well-wishers to Johnny's stall. He bent over Johnny.

"Thanks," he whispered. By now Gary Nolan and all the Red pitchers looked to Johnny when the going got tough.

As Nolan went back to his locker, Johnny flicked on a radio. "Let's get some music," he said to Pat Corrales, "some relaxing, swinging music."

He began to sing a Western song. "I like to sing. Some people tell me I have a good voice."

"Who is your favorite singer?" he was asked.

"Elvis Presley. Simon and Garfunkel. I like songs with words that have a lot of meaning."

"You could make singing another business."

Johnny stripped off his wet shirt. "Right now," he said in his pleasant Oklahoma drawl, "baseball is my business."

Johnny was working very hard in that business. In the previous year he had led the league in passed balls. And he wasn't proud that he had let all those pitches slip by him.

"I have trouble stopping low pitches," Johnny was telling Red coach Hal Smith one day.

Smith is a former catcher. "Keep your mitt closer to the grass to trap those low pitches," Smith said. In the next few days two low pitches skipped by Johnny and were ruled passed balls. In the first two months of the season a half-dozen low pitches had skidded by Johnny.

He thought about what he was doing wrong. "I've been warming up pitchers before games," he told Hal Smith. "When a pitch was in the dirt, I waved at it, didn't really try to stop it. You know, it made no difference. But that's been giving me bad habits. From now on I'm going to wear shin guards when I warm up pitchers. And I'm going to block a low pitch just as if it was a pitch in a real game."

So hard-working Johnny began to block the low pitches in warm-ups and erased the bad habit. Soon he was blocking the low pitches in games.

"Johnny is a 95 percent catcher," Dave Bristol said. "Most guys would have been content with that. But he's always working to make himself a 100 percent catcher."

Johnny nodded when he heard what Bristol had said. "I don't care if you are a consistent leader in every area," Johnny said. "For me that would include catching, throwing, handling pitchers, and hitting. Even so, you can do a little better. You should always feel you can be the best. You have got to do everything you can to make people say, 'He's the best catcher in baseball,' or whatever it is you're trying to be."

Johnny grinned. "That's what I'm working to be — the best catcher in the history of baseball."

Johnny was already acclaimed the best catcher in the National League. He was picked to start for the National League in the 1969 All-Star game. Batting against the best American League pitchers, he ripped a single and a home run. He also drew a walk in four at-bats as the National League murdered the American League, 9-3.

The Reds finished a close third in the new N.L. Western Division, trailing the Braves and Giants by only a few games. Johnny watched on television as the Eastern Division champions, the Mets, beat the Braves for the pennant and then went on to win the Series.

Johnny Bench had escaped the sophomore jinx; he had raised his standing in every batting department. He had hit 26 home runs, driven in 90 runs, and batted .293.

That winter Johnny stayed in Cincinnati to speak to fan clubs and at Little League dinners.

"I think I can hit .300," he told audiences. "I was tired in the last few weeks of the season. Catching every day takes a lot out of you. If I could play a few games at other positions during the season, I wouldn't be as tired near the end of the year."

Someone else had the same idea. That someone was Sparky Anderson, who had replaced Dave Bristol as the manager of the Reds.

"Sure," Sparky said, "catching every day takes away some of Johnny's strength as a hitter. You're taking a lot away from a man's strength when he's got to go up and down for nine innings every day. And at the same time a catcher carries a mental load — he has to concentrate on how to pitch to hitters. I'm going to take some of that physical and mental load off Johnny next season. He'll play a few games at third, first, or the outfield."

A few days before the start of spring training in 1970, Johnny was talking to his mother. The Bench family had moved to Cincinnati. Mr. and Mrs. Bench were now operating a Cincinnati

A great backstop as well as hitter, Bench makes big effort to bring down a high throw but fails to nail runner sliding home.

motel. Johnny's sister, Marilyn, was working as a secretary for a Cincinnati firm. His older brother, Ted, had moved his wife and young children to Cincinnati, where he was employed in an advertising agency; and Johnny's other brother, Bill, was selling cars in an automobile showroom in Cincinnati owned by Johnny and Pete Rose. "We Benches stick together," Johnny said to his mother.

She laughed. Then her face turned serious. "You know, Johnny," she said, "I had a dream the other night that you would drive in 125 runs this year."

He laughed. He was cocky — but not that cocky. The most runs he had ever driven in during one season was 90. His goal for 1969 was 100 RBI's and 30 home runs. "If I drove in 125 runs," Johnny told his mother, laughing, "I'd be the league's Most Valuable Player."

Johnny went to Tampa for spring training. There he played third, first, and the outfield as well as catcher. In one game he was playing third, when a batter hit a twisting liner down the left-field line. Johnny dived and snared the ball for the out.

Sparky Anderson shook his head. "It's just pitiful," he said, "that one man should have so much talent."

Johnny laughed when someone told him what

Sparky had said. "When I was sixteen I was All-State American Legion first baseman," he said in a matter-of-fact way. "When I was catching at Buffalo I used to get my rest by playing third base."

When the season began, Sparky played Johnny at first, third, and center field as well as catcher. Those "rests" seemed to help: Johnny was leading the league in homers and runs-batted-in. His average hung above .300.

The Reds were ripping the ball to all corners. Their mighty offense crushed opponents. Pete Rose dubbed the Red attack the Big Red Machine. By midseason the Big Red Machine had rolled to a huge 10-game lead in the NL West. It kept on rolling, winning the Western title by 14½ games.

The Reds smothered the Pirates in three straight games to win the play-offs and the National League pennant. Now they would take on the Baltimore Orioles in the 1970 World Series.

The phone was ringing in Johnny's apartment. Friends from Binger were calling. Could he get them World Series tickets?

A harried Johnny got all the tickets he could buy. The night before the first Series game, he tried to sleep. But he couldn't help thinking about all the World Series games he had watched on TV as a boy back in Binger. He had seen Mickey Mantle hit a home run in the last of the ninth to win a Series game against the Cardinals. Now millions of boys would be watching him on television. Johnny hoped he wouldn't disappoint anybody.

He didn't. In his first Series game Johnny slapped a single to drive in a run. But the Reds lost, 4-3. In the second game Johnny smacked a home run but again the Orioles nipped the Reds, 6-5.

In the third game Johnny rapped the ball down the third-base line. The Orioles' great third baseman, Brooks Robinson, leaped to grab the ball and throw him out. "Brooks is going to win the sports car for being the Series' best player," someone said.

Johnny owned half of a car agency. "If I'd known he wanted a car so bad," Johnny said jokingly, "I would have given him one."

The Orioles won that third game, 9-3. The Reds, short of healthy pitchers, hung on to win the next game, 6-5. A sore-armed Jim Merritt gallantly tried to start the fifth game for the Reds. The Big Red Machine handed Merritt an early lead, but he was blasted off the mound. The Orioles pounded a parade of Red pitchers to win the game, 9-3, and baseball's world championship.

Johnny had not hit as well as he wanted to in the Series — four hits in 19 at-bats for a .211 average. But he had socked one homer, driven in three runs, and thrown out three baserunners.

And for the season he had hit better than even his mother had dreamed. He had driven in 148 runs to lead the league. He had hit 45 home runs to lead the league. And he had batted .293, tying his career high.

The Sporting News named Johnny Player of the Year. And a few weeks after the season ended, Johnny was voted the National League's Most Valuable Player. At 22 he was the youngest player in big-league history to win a MVP award.

The phone was ringing incessantly in Johnny's bachelor apartment high above Cincinnati. Bob Hope wanted Johnny to appear with him on TV...could Johnny fly to Vietnam to visit the wounded...could Johnny come here...could Johnny come there...?

Yes, yes, yes, said Johnny, not knowing he was rushing down a road toward disaster.

What Johnny
Is Really Like

THE BOY was an orphan. He was visiting the Reds' clubhouse with an official of the children's welfare agency, who introduced him to the Red players.

"This is Johnny Bench," the official said.

"Glad to meet you, son," Johnny said. Johnny gave the boy an autographed ball, a bat, and a glove.

"Gee, thanks," the boy said. Then he glared at Johnny, for the boy was an unhappy Red fan. "Hey," the boy snapped, "how come you guys lost your last two games?"

Johnny laughed. In the clubhouse he enjoyed the kidding. Once Pete Rose noticed that Johnny's average had dipped 10 points in one week.

"Hey, fellows," Pete yelled one day in the club. Everyone, including Johnny, stared. "You know what Johnny Bench's new nickname is?"

"What is it?"

"Titanic," Pete said with a grin. "You know, like the ship, the Titanic, going down...."

Johnny laughed with the other players. Some people thought that Johnny and Pete would be jealous of one another, since they were the two best players on the team. Actually they admired each other's hitting and fielding. "He'll help us win a pennant," Pete said when Johnny joined the team. "He'll help us all make a lot of money."

"Pete has had a great influence on me," Johnny once told writer Earl Lawson. "Pete believes in winning, leading the league in hitting, making money. That's Pete. That's me. I want to win. I want to be the best catcher in baseball. I want to make money."

When I met Johnny for the first time, in the visitors' clubhouse in Houston, Pete introduced me to Johnny.

"I call Johnny 'Big Head,'" Pete said. "On him a cap looks like a beanie."

Johnny laughed. A little later a Red player came by as I was jotting down notes while Johnny talked. "Getting publicity, Bench?" the player asked with a grin.

Johnny looked at the player and said, "Yeah, I was just telling this reporter we ought to get rid of you, then we'd have a better team."

"What?" the player said, looking startled before he saw a grin spread across Johnny's face.

But as we talked about baseball, Johnny's face grew solemn and he seemed distant, almost unfriendly. Obviously baseball was terribly important to him and he didn't joke about it. He was 21 at the time, yet he acted like a statesman: calm, poised, certain of his answers. He chose his words carefully.

Johnny has large gray eyes that seldom seem to blink. Even when he laughs, his eyes seem to be sitting back and taking in the action, like someone watching a movie.

The next day I boarded a jetliner with the team for the flight to Cincinnati. Sitting next to Johnny, I asked him how it felt to be a baseball superstar.

He thought for several moments, staring out the window. Then, in his measured way of speaking, he said:

"Some baseball players are not aware of the power they possess. You can break hearts or make people smile, just by brushing past them or stopping and signing an autograph. I idolized athletes when I was young, so I know how people feel when they come up and they ask me for an autograph."

Several nights later we were sitting in Johnny's Cincinnati apartment. He was wearing plaid Bermuda shorts, a pink polo shirt, and a pair of battered black sneakers. Low, sleekly modern furniture filled the room. On one wall were several photographs of Johnny catching and hitting.

He stared out the window at the twinkling lights of Cincinnati stretching below us. "It's all been a dream," he was saying. "At the age of five I wished I could be a big-league ballplayer and now it's happened."

He paused. "But everything's been happening so fast. So fast."

He looked at his open palms. "I'm not complaining. I know I should have a lot of years ahead of me. I'm looking forward to them. I want to make $100,000 a year. I want to be a millionaire if I can. I want to be the greatest catcher who ever lived."

The greatest catcher who ever lived would have to throw out the fastest base stealers. I asked Johnny: "Does the pressure bother you — knowing that your pitchers expect you to throw out every base stealer?"

Johnny smiled softly. "I have what I call inner conceit," he said. "It's the feeling I have that I can throw out any baserunner alive...."

It was a wintry day in Cincinnati. In the morning Johnny played tennis on an indoor court. He had taken up the game of tennis only a few months before. Now he was drilling balls past his opponents. He hated to lose. "I'm going to be the best tennis player in the state of Ohio," he said laughing. But some people believed Johnny was serious.

Occasionally Johnny bicycled around the streets near his apartment. "Bicycling is the greatest way I know to keep in shape and get from one place to another," he told the kids who tailed after him. "A car may be faster but does nothing for your legs."

After bicycling for an hour on this winter day, Johnny stopped at a delicatessen near his apartment. The delicatessen was run by Mrs. Pia Battaglia, a graying, spectacled lady of 70. She was the mother of a former Reds' trainer.

At the delicatessen Johnny dug into Mrs. Battaglia's lasagna. "Lasagna's my favorite and she knows how to fix it," Johnny said. "She's been like a mother to me. She can't wait until I have a day off to prepare a meal for me. She also makes great steaks with mushrooms and eggs."

After lunch Johnny rode to the Reds' office where he discussed some speeches he would make to fan groups during the next few weeks. He liked making speeches. He stood up at banquets and spoke to a thousand people with the nonchalance of a Bob Hope. Big crowds didn't scare him.

Showing his versatility, Johnny Bench practices his bowling for all-around competition in TV special, "The Super Stars."

One night before a ballgame, the Reds staged a Country Music Night at Riverfront Stadium. Some 40,000 people filled most of the seats. Western singing star Bill Anderson was the host. He knew that Johnny liked to sing Western songs.

Standing at a mike near home plate, Anderson told the huge crowd: "Tommy Helms told me that if I asked Johnny Bench to sing a song, he would."

The crowd clapped for Johnny to come out and sing. In the dugout Johnny hesitated a moment or two, then he came out. He walked to the mike, picked up a guitar, and, strumming it, sang.

The crowd stood and applauded when he finished. At first some of the Red players razzed Johnny. But even they were impressed. "My wife told me that Johnny could make a million dollars as a singing star," Bernie Carbo said later.

"I'd like to make records and sing in theaters," Johnny said. "I don't have the voice for rock 'n' roll. I have more of a voice for soft ballads — the kind that tell a story. It's rock, I guess, but soft rock. But I have to take more voice lessons. Right now my voice is only good enough to sing under the shower."

A lot of young girls were hinting to Johnny that he ought to get married. He took girls out to the theater and to nightclubs. He liked to dance, and almost every night people saw a new face dancing with Johnny.

"I like a lot of girls," he once told friends. "But I don't plan to marry yet. I almost got married when I was 21. But we decided against marrying. I knew I wasn't ready.

"Basically, I'm a loner. It makes me nervous having a lot of people around me all the time. But I like to be around my family. Maybe that's because they take me as I am. They know what I'm really like. They don't treat me like a ballplayer. They treat me like a person. I don't have to put on airs with them. I'm close to my brothers and sister."

When the baseball season ends, Johnny likes

to pick up his two young nephews in his car and take them fishing. For hours they will loll in a small boat, laughing and joking while they cast, tanning themselves in the fall sunshine, and swigging soda pop.

"It doesn't really matter whether we catch anything or not. I just enjoy being with kids, and I think kids enjoy being with me," Johnny said.

He paused. "I remember when I was a kid. I copied everything I saw the big-league players do on television. That's why I always try to do things exactly right when I know kids are watching me play. I realize a lot of kids are going to be doing things the way they see me doing them during infield practice or during a game.

"I'm trying to accept the things that come with success in the right way. I try to treat people right. I try to remember I'm from a little place called Binger, Oklahoma. My dad has pointed out to me that I've already earned more money in a few years than he earned in his whole life. This is scary. I don't want to be spoiled by success.

"When I won the Rookie of the Year award in 1968," he said, "the folks back home in Binger held a Johnny Bench Day — a parade and everything. When you make the people back home feel proud of you, well, that's what it's all about...."

Johnny, Super Catcher

"WHY IS JOHNNY BENCH such a great catcher?"

Someone asked a Red pitcher that question. The pitcher pondered the question a few moments. Then he replied:

"Well, first of all he gives you a wide target. He has a wide body and he crouches low, which makes him look wider. When a catcher is wide like that, he makes the plate seem closer. When the plate seems closer, it's easier to throw strikes."

A writer once asked Sparky Anderson what made Johnny such an outstanding catcher. "Johnny does things other catchers can't do," the manager said. "We have a boy on our team, Bill Plummer, who can throw as hard as John.

But there is no one who can come up throwing quicker than John....If all our pitchers could hold a runner on first, we'd never have any bases stolen at all."

Here are some samples of Johnny's catching in action:

Lou Brock danced off first base. Cardinal slugger Joe Torre stepped in to hit. The Red pitcher, Gary Nolan, hoped Johnny would call for a curve inside. He didn't want to throw a fast ball on the outside to Torre. Big Torre murdered fast balls.

Nolan saw Johnny flick the sign: curve ball inside.

Nolan was thankful. But he knew that Johnny was taking a load on his own shoulders. Catchers like to see fast balls outside when speed merchants like Brock are on first. The catcher can mitt the ball and look down an open lane to second base. They hate to see curve balls inside with a Lou Brock breaking for second, for they have to reach down at the batter's ankles to snare the ball, then straighten up and step to the outside to throw to second.

But Johnny is a pitchers' catcher. He was calling for the best pitch for the pitcher to throw — not the easiest pitch for the catcher to catch.

Nolan snapped off an inside curve. Brock dashed for second. Torre swung and missed. Johnny gloved the ball, straightened, and threw out Brock.

"He's got more than a great arm," Brock said later. "He gets rid of the ball quick. It's amazing. One moment he has the ball — and then he doesn't."

A good catcher knows more baseball strategy than any other player on his team. "Johnny knew more about baseball at 22 than any kid I've ever met," Sparky Anderson once said. "The first time I talked to him as a manager, I was astonished at how much he knew. I never thought any 22-year-old could be that smart about baseball."

Johnny crouched behind the batter. He liked to crouch a half foot deeper than most catchers. Sure, that meant he had a half foot more to throw to second base. But he had the arm and quickness to make up for that half foot he was giving the base stealers. And by crouching a half foot deeper, Johnny could watch the batter's feet.

He saw the batter move his front foot a smidgin toward first base. "He's expecting a curve," Johnny said to himself. Johnny called for a fast ball. The batter swung feebly as the pitch blew by him for strike three.

"Johnny's thinking right along with a pitcher," Gary Nolan once said. "Like, I'll be throwing good curves on a certain day. And I know a certain hitter won't be expecting a curve ball because he is a good curve-ball hitter. I think, 'I hope John calls for the curve.' Bingo. Johnny drops two fingers for the curve ball."

Young catchers often ask Johnny for tips. "As for throwing," Johnny tells them, "you have to snap off a quicker throw to first for the pick-off because you don't have much time. When you throw to second or third, the runner has farther to go. You have a little more time to get into the throw with your arm and to release the throw. I try to throw from the top and then come down with my arm like I'm pulling down a windowshade."

On calling pitches, Johnny tells young catchers:

"Some pitchers like to call their own pitches. But if you can do a job, they will let you take charge. A catcher knows better than a pitcher what his best pitches are. A catcher can see a fast ball hop or a curve break a lot better than the pitcher can.

"In calling pitches, you have to learn what the batters can do and can't do, and what your pitcher can do and can't do. It takes concentration more than anything. You have to be thinking all the time, remembering what pitch got

First homer of the 1973 All-Star game in Kansas City is slammed by Bench in fourth inning off righty Johnny Singer.

the batter out the last time he was up. You also have to be thinking ahead. You think: If we throw him curves this time he's at bat, he'll be looking for curves the next time he's up. So the next time let's throw him fast balls. You are always trying to set the batter up. You get him to expect something and you give him something else."

Johnny called for the fast ball. Red pitcher Wayne Granger threw the fast ball. The batter, Houston's Keith Lamphard, swung and missed.

Johnny stood up and tossed the ball back to Granger. Johnny went into his crouch. He decided to signal for a curve. Then he changed his mind. The fast ball had worked once. Why not try it again? He signaled for another fast ball.

In streaked the fast ball. Lamphard swung. Johnny heard the crack of the bat and winced. He saw the ball disappear into the right-field seats. That home run won the game for the Astros.

"You make mistakes," Johnny said later. You guess wrong sometimes. Or maybe you do the right thing but the other guy beats it. You have to realize the other guys are pretty good too. You remember how the guy beats you the last time, and you try not to let it happen again.

"The catcher is the leader out there. Before every pitch the other eight guys are all looking at you. No one is looking at the second baseman or the left fielder. When the pitcher looks at me, I have to give him the confidence that I know what I'm calling. If I move a fielder a few feet to the left because I'm going to call a certain pitch, he has to believe I know what I'm doing. If the ball is hit the other way, a man is liable to say, 'C'mon John, wake up, look what you did.' A catcher has to prove himself to the ball club."

But catching has hurt him as a hitter, Johnny believes. "I know I could concentrate more on my hitting if I was playing in the outfield. A catcher is always in the game. He has to worry about the next hitter coming up and what to pitch to him. And there is always the question of the wear-and-tear physically on a catcher. I could lift my batting average 10 to 15 points a year if I could beat out infield hits. But crouching bunches up a catcher's legs and slows him down as a runner."

But Johnny always figured he could hit well enough to be among the league's best hitters.

In 1971 he got a surprise.

1971: The Road to Disaster

AFTER THE REDS won the pennant in 1970 and Johnny Bench was named the League's Most Valuable Player, an entire nation seemed to want to see him. He flew with Bob Hope to Vietnam to visit the troops. He bounced around the country to attend banquets in California, Florida, and New York. Dozens of charitable organizations begged him to appear at dinners to raise money. "Everybody has a just cause," Johnny said. "I've always been hesitant to say no."

After thousands of miles of traveling, Johnny reported to Tampa in March of 1971 for spring training. "He's exhausted," manager Sparky Anderson said. "Anyone would be exhausted after a winter like he's had."

Johnny had signed an $80,000-a-year contract. He was the highest-paid catcher in baseball. He wanted to prove he was worth the money. He wanted to crack 40 home runs. He wanted to drive in at least 125 runs. He wanted to hit .300. "I used to dream about hitting 60 home runs," he told writer Bill Libby. "As a kid that was a dream of mine. I don't think about it now. I know that's for other guys. I don't hit the ball up in the air often enough. I'm a line-drive hitter. A lot of my hits bounce off fences instead of going over them."

Johnny was standing in the dugout, gripping a bat as he talked. "I just want to be a consistent hitter whose specialty is driving in runs," he said. "I love to drive in runs. That's team play. I hate to leave men on base. I feel I've failed every time I do. I have to learn you can't do it every time. I can't let myself get discouraged."

The 1971 season began. Immediately a slump silenced the bats of the Red hitters. Tony Perez, Bernie Carbo, Lee May, and Johnny were hitting .230 and lower. The team limped along at a .500 pace — winning one, losing one.

"It's up to me," Johnny began to tell himself. "I've got to start hitting home runs if we're going to win."

He began to swing from the heels at pitches. His batting average dived even lower.

"You're trying to kill the ball," Red batting coach Ted Kluszewski told Johnny. "When you try to kill the ball, you bunch up your muscles. That slows down the speed of the bat. And it's the speed of the swing that makes a ball jump off the bat."

Pete Rose talked to Johnny. "You're trying to pull every pitch over the left-field fence for a home run," Pete told his pal. "The pitchers are throwing outside pitches to you. You're trying to pull those pitches for home runs. But all you're doing is tapping easy grounders."

"I know Pete is right," Johnny said. "A good hitter shouldn't try to pull everything. He should go with the pitch. If they pitch you inside, pull the ball. If they pitch you outside, go with the pitch and punch it to right field."

But Johnny kept on trying to jerk home runs over the left-field fence. He *had* to hit more home runs if the Big Red Machine was going to win the pennant. In one game against the Giants, Johnny hit two home runs. But the Giants won, 5-4. "Nothing seems to be going right," Johnny said. "It's frustrating, especially after we won the pennant so easily in 1970."

Johnny was swinging desperately at high pitches and low pitches. He hit a few home runs. But his batting average dipped below .220.

Opposing pitchers talked about Johnny's hitting. One day a Giant pitcher told a Cardinal pitcher: "Pitch Bench low and away. He's trying to sweep everything over the left-field fence. If you keep the ball down and away, he'll swing and strike out."

As chairman of 1973 Christmas seal drive, Johnny sells first sheet of stamps to wife of President Nixon in the White House.

In one game at Riverfront Stadium, Johnny swung at an outside pitch and missed for strike two. The pitcher flung a slider a foot from the plate. Johnny lunged at it and missed for strike three.

Cincinnati fans rained down boos as Johnny trudged back to the dugout. Johnny tried to mask his anger. He thought: These people cheered me only a year ago. Now they're booing me.

The next day the booing was like the rolling of a thousand drums as Johnny stepped to the plate. For weeks, whenever Johnny stuck his head out of the dugout, the booing bore down on him.

"I don't think anyone ever got booed at more

in one year than I did this season," Johnny was telling some friends in August. "You try to say to yourself, 'Well, the fans paid to get in, they have the right to boo.' You try to say that you don't hear it. Boy, I hear it, and it hurts...."

Johnny couldn't hide his anger any longer. "The fans were on my bandwagon last year," he said. "As soon as I slumped, they jumped off."

Well, maybe he'd give a little back. Maybe he'd stop tipping his cap to them after he hit a home run.

Johnny ended the year with a pitiful .238 average. He had hit 27 home runs, 18 fewer than he had hit in 1970. He had driven in a measly 61 runs, fewer than half of the 148 runs he had driven in a year earlier.

The Reds finished fourth in the six-team Western Division. In 1970, their pennant-winning year, the Reds had won 102 and lost 60. In this 1971 season they had won only 79 and lost 83.

The Reds asked Bench to lose a few pounds before the start of the 1972 season. "I was the same weight in 1971 as I was in 1970 when I was MVP," Johnny said with an are-you-kidding smile. But he agreed to shed a few pounds. The Reds asked him to travel to fewer banquets. Fine, said Johnny. He was glad to stay home and rest.

The Reds asked him to cut down on the time

he spent at his various businesses. Johnny and Pete Rose sold their auto agency. The Reds asked Bench if he would join a group of minor leaguers in Tampa for practice during the winter. "You could get in some hitting practice," the Reds told Johnny.

"I'd be glad to go," Johnny said. The MVP of 1970 wasn't feeling that he was too proud to go to a minor-league camp — not after that dismal 1971 season.

At Tampa Johnny sat each morning in a darkened room. He watched movies of himself hitting in 1970 and 1971. He saw a smooth hitter in 1970, an awkward hitter in 1971.

"I was trying to pull every pitch," he said, grimacing as he watched the flickering screen. "When I couldn't pull a ball, I got frustrated and swung even harder. I went on missing the ball."

After watching the movies Johnny trotted onto the field to swing at pitches thrown by minor-league pitchers. He tried to swing like the smooth swinger of 1970.

He flew home to Cincinnati after a week of practice. He was hungry for the start of spring training and the 1972 season. "I have to find out who is the real Johnny Bench — the MVP of 1970 or the one who fell flat on his face in 1971. I think I have a pretty good idea which one I am."

A few days later in talking about Johnny, his

father said, "All of the baseball greats have had bad years. John has had his. Sure it hurts. But he accepted it. It brought his feet back on the ground. He can't do everything himself. It's something he'll remember."

A month later Johnny was back in the dugout at Al Lopez field in Tampa where the Reds train. He and Pete Rose were talking with sportswriter William Leggett.

Pete spoke of a winter trade that had brought the swift second baseman, Joe Morgan, to the Reds. "And this year we got Bobby Tolan back healthy," Pete said in his energetic, fist-pumping way. "He was out all last season with an injured leg. We missed his base hits."

Pete glanced at Johnny, who was staring out at the field. "I think we got a heck of a club," Pete said. "But it won't make any difference how many hits I get, or how many hits Joe Morgan gets, or how many Bobby Tolan gets if Johnny Bench and Tony Perez don't knock us in."

Pete paused. He was looking straight at Johnny now.

"If Bench and Perez don't drive us in," Pete said, "there won't be any Big Red Machine again."

Johnny looked at Pete. In his careful way Johnny Lee Bench drawled: "Those runs *will* be driven in."

"There'll Be
No Tomorrow..."

THE 1972 SEASON BEGAN. In Johnny's first 22 times at bat, he tapped one miserable single.

Waves of booing rolled down from the stands whenever Number 5 setpped up to hit. In the stands fans waved their hands in disgust whenever Johnny popped up or struck out.

"He was a flash-in-the-pan," the fans were saying. "The pitchers have gotten wise to him. He can't hit the outside pitch. They throw the slider or fast ball outside and he can't hit it for beans."

"How about it, Johnny?" a reporter asked him one day. "You still seem to be stuck in last season's slump."

"I always get off to a slow start," Johnny replied. "There's nothing to worry about."

But Johnny *was* worried. He was hitting .246 as the Reds arrived in Houston in late May. The Reds lagged in third place, four-and-a-half games behind the first-place Astros. Johnny hoped he would start hitting in this series with Houston. This was a chance for the Reds to inch closer to first.

In the first game of the series Johnny stepped up to hit. He lashed his bat into a fast ball. The ball rocketed between the left fielder and the center fielder. They were chasing the ball toward the wall.

Johnny sped around first and toward second. He saw the ball carom off the wall and galloped to third, knees pumping. He saw the third-base coach waving him on toward home.

Johnny looped around third and ran for home — chest aching. Never in his pro career had he tried for an inside-the-park homer.

Johnny could see the Astro catcher bent, awaiting the relay throw. Johnny slid. Safe! Home run! An inside-the-park home run!

Whacking that long home run seemed to smooth out Johnny's swing. That same night he stroked a single with the bases loaded, then smacked another homer in the ninth to clinch a 9-5 Cincinnati triumph.

The next night he belted another home run — his ninth of the year. "Man, I haven't felt this good in two years," Johnny told Pete Rose after the game.

"Johnny's looking more like his old self," manager Sparky Anderson whispered to one of his coaches. "And that sure makes me happy."

Johnny made Sparky even happier the next night. He lined a single that started a Red rally. The Reds beat the Astros, 9-3. A few days later he lofted his second home run of the game, this time in the 17th inning, to beat the Phils, 6-3. It was Cincinnati's sixth straight victory.

Johnny had now blasted seven home runs in five games. That tied a National League record set way back in 1929.

Johnny wasn't finished. In 51 at-bats he clipped 21 hits to raise his batting average to .306. In those 51 times at bat he had slugged nine homers and driven in 24 runs. That streak of hitting had helped to lift the Reds to first place.

The team flew home to be greeted by 2,000 cheering fans at the airport. When Johnny Bench stepped out of the plane, the fans let out a special roar. He waved. The boos of yesterday were the cheers of today.

A few days later Johnny drove his 16th home run of the season into the left-field seats at Riverfront Stadium. He trotted around the bases. The fans were standing and applauding. So far

Bench receives award from Baseball Commissioner Bowie Kuhn for greatest number of fan votes in 1973 all-star balloting.

this season Johnny had not tipped his hat after hitting a home run.

Now he was trotting toward the dugout. The noise of the fans grew like a deluge. Johnny looked up at the stands. He hesitated. Then he tipped his hat.

The rest of the Western Division could not stop the Big Red Machine. The pitchers could not stop Johnny Bench. He played catcher, third base, first base, and all the positions in the outfield. But wherever he played, he hit. Near the end of the season he led the league in runs-batted-in.

"I'd also like to beat out Nate Colbert for the home-run title," Johnny said in late September. He and San Diego slugger Nate Colbert were separated by only a few home runs. Then Johnny triggered a burst of round-trippers. He hit more home runs in the month of September than the entire Pittsburgh Pirate team hit. Johnny won the home-run title with 40 to Colbert's 38.

Bench had also driven in 125 runs to beat out Chicago's Billy Williams, who drove in 122. Billy had hit .333 to lead the National League. Johnny had batted .270, a big leap over his .238 of a year earlier. But Johnny and a lot of people thought that Billy Williams would be picked as the league's MVP. After all, Billy had led the league in hitting, had finished second in runs-batted-in, and third in home runs (with 37).

Red fans argued that Johnny should be the MVP. He'd led his team on defense with his arm, and on offense with his bat, they pointed out.

Johnny Bench had only one thought: Beat the Bucs.

That was the Red slogan as the play-offs began between the Reds and the Pirates for the National League pennant.

"Being in the World Series," Johnny said, "that's what every baseball season is all about."

The Pirates won the first game, 5-1. The Reds won the second game, 5-3, to tie the playoffs at one game apiece. In Cincinnati the Pirates won the third game, 3-2. If the Pirates won the next game, they would be the National League champions.

"We've got our backs to the wall," Johnny said to a writer in the dugout before the fourth game. "If we lose, the season's all over. There's no tomorrow."

The Reds came to bat in the bottom of the first inning. With two out and Bobby Tolan on first base, Johnny rammed a single over second base. Tolan zipped around to third base.

Tony Perez stepped in. Johnny edged off first

base, watching the young Pirate pitcher, Dock Ellis. On the pitch to the plate Johnny took off for second base. He didn't try to steal very often, so he had surprised Ellis and catcher Manny Sanguillen.

Sanguillen threw hurriedly to second. The ball skipped by the second baseman and bounded into center field. Bobby Tolan trotted home and the Reds led 1-0 in their no-tomorrow, do-or-die game.

Johnny came up to hit again in the fourth inning. The score was still 1-0. He punched a single. And again he took off for second on a pitch. He slid into second a hair ahead of the throw from Sanguillen for his second stolen base of the game.

With two out, Cesar Geronimo skied a high pop over shortstop. Pirate shortstop Gene Alley circled under the ball. Johnny was running all the way, not assuming that Alley would catch the pop. And he didn't. Alley dropped the ball, and Johnny scored to put the Reds ahead, 2-0.

The Reds went on to win 7-1. The play-off was tied at two games each. There would be a tomorrow in which the Reds — or the Pirates — would win the National League pennant.

In that final game of the play-offs, in the ninth inning, the Pirates were ahead 3-2. The Cincinnati fans in Riverfront Stadium were standing and roaring for a rally as Johnny Bench came up to lead off the last of the ninth. His mother came down to the railing behind home plate to plead with her son to hit a home run.

And Johnny hit that home run, a dramatic shot into the right-field seats, and the Reds went on to win the game and the pennant.

Later, amid the pandemonium in their clubhouse, Red coach Ted Kluszewski marveled over that homer:

"I don't know of any other right-handed hitter in the league who has the strength to blast an outside pitch like that into the right-field seats," the mountainous Klu said. "You have to be tremendously strong to go with an outside pitch and drive it almost 400 feet."

Reporters ringed Johnny. "He was telling them how his mother had called for him to hit the home run.

"Do you always do what your mother tells you?" a reporter asked.

"I try to," Johnny Bench said, grinning.

"Don't Let Johnny Bench Beat You with His Bat…"

THE 1972 WORLD SERIES opened in Cincinnati. Johnny's phone was ringing day and night. Everyone wanted tickets.

"I wish we had opened on the road," he told a writer. "At home the phones never stop ringing. Everyone wants to visit you. Friends and family want to see you before the game. Everybody means well. But it's just a little too much. And that creates a lot of stress.

"There's always some nervousness before the first game. You realize how important everything is —I guess the pressure also comes from psyching yourself up to get ready for the biggest effort of the season. The big thing is to try to relax and play baseball the way you know you can play."

The Oakland A's had won the American League pennant. Their scouts had been watching the Reds closely for weeks. Before the first game the Oakland scouts talked to their pitchers:

"The Reds do most of their scoring by getting one of their first three hitters — Rose, Morgan, or Tolan — on base. Then Johnny Bench drives them home. If you can keep Rose, Morgan, and Tolan off the bases, Bench won't have anyone to drive home."

The scouts said they knew how to pitch to Rose, Morgan, and Tolan. "Throw the fast ball," they told their pitchers. "Then come back with a slow change-up, and you can get them out."

But the scouts could spot no weakness in Bench. "Don't give him a good fast ball," they warned. "He'll kill it. Throw him breaking pitches — but keep them low and away. Don't throw strikes to him. If you walk him, he hasn't hurt you."

And then the scouts stressed this final point: "If at all possible, don't let Bench beat you with his bat."

In the first two games of the Series the Oakland strategy worked perfectly. The A's pitchers put down Rose, Tolan, and Morgan with change-ups. They were never on base. Johnny came up six different times in those two games and looked at empty bases. He smacked three hits in those six at-bats, but his hits were wasted. They might have driven in runs that would have won both games. The A's won the first game, 3-2, and the second, 2-1.

Pete Rose snarled, "Morgan and Tolan and I have got to get on base. We can't win this Series if Johnny is hitting with nobody on."

The Reds won the third game, 1-0, with help from the bottom of their batting order. In the fourth game Johnny smashed two hits in four at-bats and he stole a base. But Rose, Morgan, and Tolan collected only one hit among them. The Reds lost, 3-2, and trailed in the series three games to one. If they lost the fifth game, again there would be no tomorrow.

The Reds went into the last of the ninth ahead 5-4. If they could get three more outs, there would at least be one more tomorrow.

The huge crowd in Oakland was roaring for the A's to come back and win the world championship at home. The din was ear-shattering. The A's had runners on first and third with only one out. A long hit would win the game and the championship.

The toothpick-slim Campy Campaneris stood at the plate. Crouching behind Campy, Johnny eyed Blue Moon Odom, an Oakland pinch

Bench plays role of peacemaker, right foreground, as he holds buddy Pete Rose after fight with the Mets' Bud Harrelson.

runner, inching off third base. Johnny knew that Odom was fast. He'd try to score, even on a short fly ball. If he scored, the game was tied.

Johnny called for a fast ball. It streaked homeward. Campaneris swung and Johnny watched the ball arch upward toward first base.

Second baseman Joe Morgan was running toward the foul line. He waved off first baseman Tony Perez. Morgan caught the ball on the grass in foul territory.

Johnny saw Odom flying toward home and blocked the plate. He looked for the throw from Morgan. But Morgan, starting to throw, slipped on the grass. He recovered and threw. Odom was now bearing down on home. But Johnny stood his ground, grabbed the throw, and tagged him out.

The game was over. The Reds were the 5-4 winners. They now trailed three games to two. They had to win or tie the sixth game or, again, for them there would be no tomorrow.

The two teams flew back to Cincinnati. "Let's get an early lead in tomorrow's game," Johnny told the other Reds. Vida Blue was pitching for the A's. When Blue got an early lead, his fast ball seemed to sizzle even faster.

The sixth game was scoreless when Johnny came up in the fourth inning. Then Vida Blue threw the fast ball, and Johnny rammed it high into the left-field seats for a home run and a 1-0 Red lead.

In the A's dugout manager Dick Williams frowned. *Don't let Bench beat you with his bat,* the scouts had warned.

Williams turned toward his pitchers. "Walk Bench if you have to," he growled. "Don't let him swing at strikes."

Johnny walked twice in the game and scored twice. The Reds were easy 8-1 winners.

Now the Series was down to the seventh and final game. In the first inning Red center fielder Bobby Tolan misjudged a line drive. It soared over his head and bounced against the center-field wall for a triple. The next batter, Gene

Tenace, slapped a hopper at third baseman Denis Menke. The ball hit something and bad-hopped over Menke's head. The runner scored from third and the A's led on two fluke hits, 1-0.

The Reds fought back to tie the game in the fifth, 1-1. Then the A's came back with two runs in the top of the sixth to go ahead 3-1.

The Reds came to bat in the eighth still trailing 3-1. Pete Rose led off. He timed a change-up perfectly and lined a single. Joe Morgan leaned into another change-up and slashed the ball down the right-field line. Rose sped to third and Morgan galloped into second with a double.

The next batter popped up. Coming to the plate was Johnny Bench. The Cincinnati fans were on their feet. Their thundering filled the stadium. *Come through just one more time, Johnny. Come through with one more hit that will tie this game. Come through with one more home run that could win this game and the World Series.*

Manager Dick Williams of the A's stepped out of the dugout and called time. He walked slowly toward the mound.

Don't let Bench beat you with his bat....

Atop the mound Williams looked at pitcher Rollie Fingers. "Walk Bench intentionally," Williams told his pitcher.

The pitcher stared for a moment. Walk Bench

intentionally? That would load the bases. And if Johnny was able to score he would put the Reds ahead, 4-3. He was the winning run. A basic rule in baseball is never put the winning run on base intentionally.

Williams was breaking that rule. "Bench might beat us with his legs by coming around to score from first," Williams said to one of his coaches when he returned to the dugout. "But never am I going to let him beat us with his bat."

Fingers walked Johnny intentionally, filling the bases. Tony Perez lofted a fly to score one run, but Denis Menke tapped an easy fly for the last out. Williams' strategy had worked. Johnny Bench had not gotten the chance to beat the A's.

Oakland held off the Reds in the bottom of the ninth and ran joyfully to their clubhouse, 3-2 winners and world champions.

Six of the seven games in the 1972 World Series had been decided by a single run — a Series record. It was probably the most closely contested Series in history. Both managers said the same thing: "Either team could have won, the Series was that close."

For days afterward Johnny couldn't shake off his disappointment. *If only there had been runners on base when he had socked those hits in the first two games...he might have driven in*

*runs that would have won those games.
If...if...if....*

"We were within one measly single of winning the Series in the eighth inning of that last game," he said. "But you have to give the A's' pitchers credit. They stopped us when they had to stop us."

Johnny figured he would soon run head-on into another disappointment. He hoped to win the 1972 Most Valuable Player Award. But when he read that *The Sporting News* had named Billy Williams the Player of the Year, he was sure that the nation's sportswriters would also pick him as the MVP.

The writers, however, picked Johnny Bench as the MVP. He had been voted MVP for the second time in three years.

Johnny got the news at his Cincinnati apartment. He smiled, remembering the boos and frustrations of 1971. "It's always satisfying to come back," he said.

He had come back from a batting slump. Within a few weeks he would have to come back from something much more serious.

"The Greatest
Catcher Ever…"

THE DOCTOR looked at Johnny. Then he glanced again at the X ray he had been studying. "You have a small spot on the lung, Johnny," the doctor said.

All the Reds had been X-rayed during a physical checkup before the World Series. When the doctors examined Johnny's X rays, they saw a spot, about the size of a marble, on his right lung.

"It's probably nothing harmful," the doctor was telling Johnny. "We'll operate and cut it out. Then we'll examine it. But there is always the possibility it could be malignant."

Johnny knew what that meant. He could have cancer of the lung. Sometimes lung cancer can be cured. Sometimes it can't and the patient dies.

For weeks he worried about the coming operation. "I've been telling myself all along that anything could happen to end my career," Johnny told friends. "I could get injured, get sick. Then it's all over."

A few days before the operation Johnny's mother was talking with one of her friends. "He's nervous, but he isn't going to let it show," she said.

Johnny entered Cincinnati's Christ Hospital. The day before the operation, his father came to see him.

Resting in bed, Johnny smiled at his father. "Dad," he said, "I'll be behind the plate when the season starts."

"And he'll be there," his father said that night to a reporter. "He's quite a guy."

The next day Johnny was wheeled into the operating room. He looked at the doctor, Dr. Luis Gonzalez, and grinned. "Get on with it," he said.

An hour later the surgeons had cut out the spot. It was placed under microscopes. Within minutes Johnny's family heard the news: The spot was not cancerous. Johnny would be all right.

During the next few days some 10,000 letters

addressed to Johnny Bench flooded the hospital mail room. When he was able to sit up, his mother showed him some of the letters.

"This is nothing short of miraculous," Johnny told reporters. "People I don't know, all of them wishing me good luck and telling me they're looking forward to seeing me behind the plate."

In baseball, however, some of the managers, coaches, and players were wondering if the operation had sapped Johnny's strength. Could he hit as hard? Could he throw as hard?

Ten days after the operation Johnny walked slowly out of the hospital. "I feel a little empty on the right side, where the surgery was performed," he said.

A few weeks later he flew to Florida to compete in a kind of "mini Olympics" with stars from other sports. He would bowl and play tennis and bike against the likes of Johnny Unitas, pole vaulter Bob Seagren, and race-car driver Peter Revson. Bob Seagren was the eventual winner of the competition.

Before the events began, however, Johnny, Revson, and Seagren, in a friendly competition of their own, were hitting baseballs thrown by a pitching machine. Johnny was popping the ball onto the infield grass. Seagren and Revson whacked 300-foot liners.

"We had a three-man hitting contest,"

Johnny said later with a rueful grin. "I finished third behind a pole vaulter and a racing-car driver."

Whispers ran through the big-league camps as spring training began: Johnny has lost his power. He can't throw. Johnny had signed a 1973 contract for $100,000, the most money ever paid to a catcher. The whispers said he wasn't worth a nickel.

In spring training runners stole bases on him. "Runners want to go on the first pitch," wrote one reporter, "because they're so sure they can steal on Bench. He can't throw anymore."

"Bench is physically sound," insisted Sparky Anderson. "Naturally, he has to wait awhile to get his arm in shape."

The 1973 season began. The Reds met the Giants. The Giants' young Garry Maddox was being hailed as the fastest man in the game. Maddox had heard the stories about Johnny's weakened arm. Now he was going to challenge that arm. He danced off first base. The Giant and Red players leaned forward in their dugouts, anxious to see the outcome of this duel.

The Red pitcher glanced toward Maddox, then threw to the plate. Maddox was already halfway to second.

Johnny grabbed the inside pitch, straightened, and threw.

Bench leaps on home plate after hitting game-winning home run in first game of 1973 National League playoff with Mets.

Shortstop Dave Concepcion dashed to the bag and saw the ball zipping toward him a foot off the ground. It thudded into the pocket of his glove, and he slapped the glove on the sliding Maddox.

Out! signaled the umpire.

A few weeks later San Diego manager Don Zimmer was talking to a reporter. "I read all spring that the operation had weakened Bench's throwing arm. This morning I look at the records and I see that five guys have tried to steal against him and he has thrown out all five. To me he throws as hard as he ever did."

But Johnny wasn't banging any home runs. Pitchers were telling each other you could throw fast balls right by Johnny Bench. "He's not as strong or as quick with the bat," the pitchers were saying.

"I know what the trouble is," Johnny was telling Ted Kluszewski. "It's the same trouble I had in 1971. I'm swinging too hard. I'm trying to kill the ball."

"That's right," Klu said. "Just concentrate on meeting the ball."

In June the Reds flew to New York to play the Mets. Pitching for the Mets was their ace 20-game winner, Tom Seaver. When Johnny strode to the plate in the first inning, the 20,000 New York fans, most of them rooting for the Mets, applauded Johnny. The applause was their way of welcoming him back after his surgery. But after the applause died down, the Mets' fans rooted for Seaver to strike him out.

Seaver did strike him out. He struck out nine Reds in the first five innings. "He has great stuff tonight," Johnny said to a Red player in the dugout between innings. "I don't think I've ever seen him faster."

The Mets led, 1-0, as the Reds came to bat in the top of the sixth inning. Seaver struck out the first Red hitter — his 10th strikeout of the night.

Johnny Bench was the next hitter. "You're hitting all the way," Sparky Anderson had said to him as he left the dugout. Johnny nodded. He knew what Sparky meant. He had permission to swing at any pitch — even if the count was three balls and no strikes.

Seaver threw a fast ball outside. Ball one. Another fast ball outside. Ball two. A slider broke inside. Ball three.

Johnny knew that Seaver wasn't giving up. He was still trying to strike him out. *Fast Ball,* Johnny figured. He'll be throwing the fast ball.

Johnny dug in. He saw the fast ball zipping toward him at maybe 100 miles an hour. Johnny swung, meeting the ball belt-high. The loud *crack!* told him and the crowd all they needed to know. Home run!

Johnny jogged the bases. He was smiling to himself. That swing had felt good. He had tried to connect with the ball, tried to make contact. He hadn't tried to kill it. And the ball had sailed right out of the park.

The game was tied, 1-1, and the Reds went on to beat Seaver and the Mets, 4-1.

That home run loosened up Johnny's swing. The team went to Philadelphia. Pitching for the Phils was Steve Carlton, acclaimed the best pitcher in the league in 1972.

Johnny whacked a home run in his first at-bat. He hit a home run his second time up, and he hit a home run his third time up. Since he had hit a home run in his last at-bat the night before, he had now smacked four homers in four successive at-bats, tying a big-league record held by players like Lou Gehrig and Mickey Mantle.

After the game Johnny talked to reporters. His face was solemn. He had put on a wide-lapeled blue knit suit, a blue-flowered sports shirt, and black boots.

Yes, Johnny said, he knew he was leading the league in runs-batted-in. "I'm out of my slump," Johnny said with a grin. "All I have to learn to do is not to try so hard. Just make contact. That's the secret."

Pete Rose was standing in another corner of the dressing room. He jerked a thumb toward Johnny. "When Johnny Bench is hitting," Pete said, "this team is twice as good a ball club."

Johnny smiled when he heard what Pete had said. "I don't know about that," Johnny said. "But I do like having the other guys depend on me. If you have an object in life you shouldn't be afraid to stand up and say what it is. My object is to be the greatest catcher ever to play the game."

Late in June the Reds trailed the Dodgers by 11 games in the NL West. The Red pitchers were giving up runs faster than the Red batters could score them.

Then Jack Billingham began to hurl shutouts. The other Red pitchers turned stingy in giving up runs. The Reds won 50 of the last 70 games to catch the Dodgers and finish first. "We refused to roll over and play dead," Johnny told friends.

Facing the Mets in the NL playoff in the first game, the Mets led, 1-0, in the eighth inning. New York's Tom Seaver was flinging "steam heat," as the hitters call good fastballs. Then Pete Rose hit a home run to tie the score, 1-1. In the last of the ninth Bench came to bat. "He'll try to throw a fastball past me like he usually does," Johnny told himself. He was right. Johnny lined it over the leftfield fence for a home run and a 2-1 Red victory.

The playoffs came down to a fifth and final game. Seaver was again pitching for the Mets. In the first inning, Reds stood on second and third, only one out. Tony Perez stepped in to hit. "I've got to strike him out," Seaver told his catcher. "Then we can walk Bench. There's no way I want to pitch to Bench with runners on second and third."

Seaver struck out Perez. He walked Bench intentionally. Then he retired young Ken Griffey on a pop-up to end the inning.

The Mets went on to win the game, 7-2, and the pennant. A disappointed Johnny Bench went home. But as he got ready for the 1974 season, Johnny could look back on a year in which he had attained the goal he seeks each season: driving in a lot of runs. His .253 average and 25 home runs had driven in 104 runs for the Reds, best on the team and third best in the National League.

After that final game of the season, "Johnny Cool" picked up his satchel containing his spikes and glove and started for the door. Beyond that door stretched a good part of a long career in baseball. And at the end of that career, a door most likely will swing open and he will walk into The Hall of Fame—just as Ted Williams had predicted. For in the eyes of many experts who have seen him cut down base stealers and swat home runs, Johnny Lee Bench is already one of the greatest catchers ever to play the game.